Go Within So You Don't Go Without:

Master Your Mind, Conquer Adversity, and Live Fearlessly

SHANNON V. DOUGLAS

Resilient Publishing

ISBN: 979-8-218-35943-0

Printed in the United States of America

DEDICATION

To the seekers of inner light,
May these words guide you through the shadows,
Igniting the flame within and revealing the strength you've always possessed.
This book is a tribute to your resilience and authenticity,
A celebration of the power you hold to redefine your narrative.
In dedication to the unwavering spirit that shapes the journey,
May these pages be a compass for your unique path.
With heartfelt admiration and gratitude,

Shannon Douglas

CONTENTS

Introduction   vi

Preface   viii

Acknowledgments   ix

Chapter 1   THE MIRROR OF SELF-REFLECTION   Pg 1

Chapter 2   WHAT IS UP WITH YOU?   Pg 4

Chapter 3   WHAT'S THE MATTER AND WHY DOES IT MATTER   Pg 8

Chapter 4   WHAT DO YOU BELIEVE ABOUT YOURSELF?   Pg 11

Chapter 5   THE POWER OF SETTING INTENTIONS AND TAKING ACTION   Pg 15

Chapter 6   YOU NEED TO SAY "FK IT" AND FACE IT**   Pg 19

Chapter 7   THE ART OF BEING SOULFISH   Pg 22

Chapter 8   UNLEASH YOUR INNER RESILIENCE   Pg 25

Chapter 9   UNLEASH YOUR SELF-COMPASSION WARRIOR   Pg 28

Chapter 10   THE MAESTRO OF YOUR EXISTENCE   Pg 32

Chapter 11   THE POWER OF BOUNDARIES   Pg 35

Chapter 12   UNLEASHING YOUR INNER POWER   Pg 39

Chapter 13   THE POWER OF GRATITUDE: CULTIVATING APPRECIATION   Pg 42
             IN DAILY LIFE

Chapter 14   THE WISDOM OF REFLECTION: UNVEILING SELF-DISCOVERY   Pg 46
             THROUGH INTROSPECTION

Chapter 15   LIMITLESS FREEDOM PRACTICES   Pg 49

Chapter 16	EMPOWER YOUR FUTURE: A BLUEPRINT FOR RENEWAL AND PLANNING	Pg 53
Chapter 17	AFFIRMATIONS FOR TRANSFORMATION	Pg 57
	REFLECTIONS AND QUESTIONS	Pg 62
	A LETTER TO THE FUTURE SELF	Pg 65
	DISCUSSION QUESTIONS FOR BOOK CLUBS	Pg 67
	About The Author	Pg 70

Introduction

Embrace Your Current State

To completely embrace and become the change you want to become and see in the mirror, you cannot ignore where and who you are today. Embrace where you are at this very moment. I do not care if you are grateful and thankful or sad and disappointed. Embrace where you are today because you want to ensure that you are fully aware of how you got here in the first place! Seriously, do not continue to lie to yourself and play yourself short. Do not continue telling yourself the same crap about how you are going to change this and that about yourself and poof another year goes by, if you are blessed to see another year. For that very reason you should want to do something different to feel different. Do something extraordinary to be extraordinary.

I do not know about you but there comes a time in one's life when you simply become fed up with the current state of your life and feel like doing something about it. The operative word here is doing. Understand that your life's journey can be a damn good trip if you make it so. Yes you! Quite frankly no one else is going to do anything as good for you as you would, unless you are simply self-negligent. One day I googled the word negligent and according to the Google dictionary the adjective negligent is defined as "failing to take proper care in doing something." Hmmmm, so to be self-negligent is failing to take proper care of yourself!

To continue this roll that we're on I then looked up self-neglect and Wikipedia pops up with the following definition, "Self-neglect is a behavioral condition in which an individual neglects to attend to their basic needs, such as personal hygiene, appropriate clothing, feeding, or tending appropriately to any medical conditions they have.[1] More generally, any lack of self-care in terms of personal health, hygiene and living conditions can be referred to as self-neglect." That in itself is pretty deep. For that reason, we need to establish or for those of you who are in progress with paying attention to yourselves reestablish.

In the following chapters we will explore your life's journey up to this point and get a better understanding of where you're headed. To make this exploration an effective one you need to come equipped with an open mind and a willingness to be REAL with YOURSELF. These two wonderful things will serve you well on your exploration if you use them. That even means take a moment or five to forget about the other books you have read or the advice you have received from family and friends to make your life a better one. Why do you ask? Well because we are talking about you! No one else but you. Who knows more about you than you? You are the source of your truth and the author of your story, so why not start there. You are the most knowledgeable about your life's experiences so make certain that the experiences you have going forward are wonderful and fruitful.

I challenge you to GO WITHIN SO YOU DON'T GO WITHOUT.

Preface

Welcome to the heart of transformation. "Go Within So You Don't Go Without" is more than a book; it is your passport to a fearless journey of self-discovery. Get ready for a no-nonsense exploration of resilience, authenticity, and unshakable self-awareness.

This book is your companion through inner sanctuaries, the rhythmic dance of life, and the profound stillness that reveals your true essence. It's not just a guide; it is a toolkit, packed with practical exercises, profound reflections, and a symphony of wisdom to unlock your dormant potential.

In these pages, you will confront your doubts, name your fears, and turn failures into stepping stones. This isn't a fairytale; it's your gritty war epic. You will break free from self-imposed limitations and craft your anthem of resilience.

Join the journey filled with personal narratives, universal truths, and the collective wisdom of those who've triumphed in self-discovery. To those who inspired and challenged me, I express gratitude. To you, dear reader, I extend an open hand, inviting you to discover strength, insights, and guidance for your unique journey. This book is a lantern lighting up the vast landscapes within you. Get ready to uncover the power that lies beneath the surface.

Anticipating your transformation,

Shannon D

ACKNOWLEDGMENTS

As I reflect on the journey of creating this book, I am filled with gratitude for the many individuals who have played pivotal roles in its realization. Writing these pages has been a transformative experience, and I owe my deepest thanks to those who have supported and inspired me along the way.

First and foremost, I extend my heartfelt appreciation to my family—your unwavering encouragement and understanding have been my pillars of strength. To my friends and mentors, your wisdom and guidance have illuminated my path, shaping the narrative of this work.

To the readers and supporters of my work, I am truly grateful for your enthusiasm and engagement. Your presence on this journey has given purpose to the words on these pages.

Last but not least, I express my immense gratitude to the universe, which conspired in mysterious ways to bring this project to fruition.

Thank you, one and all, for being a part of this incredible voyage.

With sincere appreciation,

Shannon Douglas

CHAPTER 1
THE MIRROR OF SELF-REFLECTION

"You have to find your own truth. You have to find what truly works for you, because I think there's a lot of advice out there, and people can actually be giving the right advice, but it's not necessarily right for you." - Jay Z

Hello there, my fellow journeyer, and welcome to the first chapter of "Go Within so you Don't Go Without." I'm Shannon Douglas, your guide on this transformative expedition into the depths of self-awareness and personal growth. I love those words from Jay Z because not only are they true but are what I see as some of the ingredients in a successful transformation recipe in your life. If you want true transformation, you must remember it starts and ends with YOU. Have you ever stood in front of a mirror and truly looked at your reflection? I mean, really gazed into your own eyes, and acknowledged the person staring back at you? It might sound like a simple act, but it's astonishing how many of us rush through life without ever taking the time to do just that.

In this chapter, we are diving headfirst into the power of self-reflection. You see, the journey to becoming the change you want starts right here, in the mirror. Whether you're feeling grateful and thankful for where you are today or grappling with sadness and disappointment, the first step is to embrace your current state without judgment. It is easy to fool ourselves, to tell ourselves we'll change this or that about our lives, and then, poof, another year slips away. Being aware of that fact immediately places you in a better position. But you cannot forget that we're here for something different, something extraordinary. There comes a time when we've had enough of the same old story, when we yearn for transformation, not just making a difference but being and doing different and the operative word here is "doing." You hold the reins to your life's journey, and it can be an incredible adventure if you choose to make it so. Trust me; no one else is going to care for you as well as you can, unless you're neglecting yourself. I once looked up the word "negligent" and found that it means "failing to take proper care in doing something." So, to be self-negligent is to fail to take proper care of yourself. It goes even deeper when you explore self-neglect, a condition where individuals neglect their basic needs, from personal hygiene to health. It's time to establish, or for those already on this path, reestablish a connection with yourself.

In the upcoming chapters, we'll embark on a journey through your life up to this point. We'll gain a deeper understanding of where you've been and where you're headed. To make this exploration truly effective, you'll need an open mind and a willingness to be brutally honest with yourself. So, my fellow traveler, are you ready to look into that mirror and start this transformative journey? Remember, the first step is embracing your current self, no matter where you stand. Let's go within to discover the extraordinary person waiting to emerge. Stay tuned for the next chapter, where we'll delve even deeper into the power of authenticity and being true to yourself.

Chapter 1 Exercise: Confront Your Reality

Alright, if you are serious, recognize that it is time to cut the crap and get real with yourself. This exercise is not for the faint of heart; it's for the warriors ready to face the music. No sugarcoating, no excuses.

Reality Check Journaling: Grab a notebook, and every day, write down three things that didn't suck about your day. I don't care if it was just that your coffee was hot. Find the silver lining, and jot it down. It's time to shift your focus, even if it's just a bit.

Life Map Showdown: Draw that life map, but don't just mark the highs; highlight the lows, the struggles, the battles you've faced. Stare at it. Own it. This map is your battlefield, and you're still standing. Remember that.

Mirror Wake-Up Call: Stand tall in front of that mirror. Look yourself dead in the eyes, and spill the truth. Talk about your dreams, your excuses, your reality. This ain't a therapy session; it's a wake-up call. No more lies. It's time to face the person staring back at you. This exercise ain't about coddling, it's about shaking yourself awake. Embrace the discomfort, confront your reality head-on.

This is the gritty work, the foundation of your transformation. You're not here for mediocrity, you're here to kick ass and take names. Now get to it.

CHAPTER 2
WHAT IS UP WITH YOU?

"The truth may hurt, but fooling yourself will enslave you." -
Charles F. Glassman

Welcome back to our journey of self-discovery. In this chapter, we're going to dig deep into the questions that matter: What is up with you? How real are you with yourself? How honest are you with yourself? How well do you truly know yourself? We often claim to be masters of self-awareness, champions of authenticity, and experts on our own lives. Yet, despite these claims, why do so many of us struggle to find consistent happiness in our daily existence? The answer lies in the comfort of routine and the complacency that can settle in when we fail to pay attention to our own level of consciousness.

Take a moment to reflect: Do you have brilliant ideas that never see the light of day? Are you dissatisfied with your body? Does a relationship in your life leave you feeling unfulfilled? Are you stuck in a job that offers no room for growth? Do you find yourself trapped in a perpetual state of depression? Is life overwhelming, leaving you feeling powerless to change it? Do you believe that your life cannot improve, regardless of whether you feel good or bad about it? If you've answered yes to any of these questions, please know that you are not alone. I've been there too, and I share this not to console you by saying that others are unhappy as well, but to assure you that you don't have to remain in this state.

There is a light at the end of life's tunnel, and it's not a freight train destined to destroy you. Let's be clear; I won't sugarcoat it. I won't tell you there's a magic potion for instant transformation because there isn't. While some may seek temporary fixes, it often leads to addiction and a sense of brokenness. You may know this path all too well, having experienced it or perhaps currently navigating it.

The reality is this: Change is not easy. It's not a snap of the fingers or a sip of a potion. Many of us have heard uplifting, optimistic advice that should lead us to success and happiness, but we remain trapped in a cycle of negativity and self-doubt. We tell ourselves destructive stories, like, "I've been here so long, nothing will change," or "I'll never get that promotion." The problem often lies in our closed minds, minds that reject perspectives that challenge our core beliefs about ourselves. We must realize that we are not our thoughts; we are the ones experiencing those thoughts, the emotions they stir, and the moments they impact.

This is why maintaining a high level of self-awareness is crucial. A closed mind is a wasted mind. Don't underestimate it; it can take control if you let it. You must understand that you are not your thoughts; you have the power to control them. Step out of those negative conversations in your head and increase your self-awareness by examining your emotions. Why do I feel guilty even though I've been forgiven? Why am I stuck in a career I dislike? Am I wasting my talents? A closed mind is limiting, putting a ceiling on your potential when, in reality, the sky's the limit. Worse, a closed mind can breed self-destructive thoughts, damaging your consciousness.

Consider this: In medicine, treating symptoms is different from curing the condition. Just as painkillers alleviate symptoms but don't heal bones, scratching the surface of your issues with quick fixes won't lead to lasting change. So, what do you do when you're faced with problems? Do you address only the symptoms, or do you delve deeper to identify the root causes? It's time to give yourself the space to think. Your life depends on it.

Fixing surface-level symptoms might provide temporary relief, but it guarantees that your problems will return, often worse than before. Instead, let's examine the causes of your issues. Look at why something happened and what happened as a result. We often focus solely on outcomes, but it's time to shift our focus to causality. To truly transform your life, you'll need to dig deeper than ever before. Scratching the surface won't suffice; it reinforces the mess rather than eliminating it.

So, are you ready to roll up your sleeves and dig deep? Let's embark on this journey together, to confront the truths about ourselves and discover the keys to lasting happiness and personal growth. Stay tuned for the next chapter, where we'll explore the power of authenticity and being true to yourself.

Chapter 2 Exercise: Unmask Your Truth

Alright, rockstar, it's time to strip away the bullcrap and get to the raw truth. This exercise is for those ready to cut through the self-deception and embrace reality like a warrior.

Brutal Self-Inventory: List out the areas of your life where you are fooling yourself. Be brutally honest. Are you slacking at work? Ignoring your health? Hiding from your true feelings in a toxic relationship? Write it down, no matter how uncomfortable it feels.

Reality Check Questions: Answer the hard-hitting questions. Get real about your happiness, your body, your relationships, your career. Ask yourself: "Am I just coasting through life?" "What am I truly unhappy about?" "Where am I settling?" Confront each question with the ferocity of a lion hunting its prey.

Flip the Script: Identify one negative belief you have been clinging to. Maybe it's "I'm not good enough" or "I can't change." Now, flip that script. Write down the opposite, empowering belief. This is your new mantra. Repeat it daily, and watch the transformation unfold. No more hiding, no more pretending. This exercise is your truth serum, and it's time to gulp it down.

Embrace the discomfort, stare your excuses in the face, and unmask the real you. The journey to extraordinary begins with unwavering truth. Let's roll.

CHAPTER 3
WHAT'S THE MATTER AND WHY DOES IT MATTER

"Life is like riding a bicycle. To keep your balance, you must keep moving." - Albert Einstein

Welcome back, my fellow explorers, as we journey deeper into the realms of self-discovery. In this chapter, we're going to confront the emotions that often plague us: anger, sadness, disappointment, hatred, irritation, and all their kin.

Have you ever noticed how these feelings can consume you, much like jumping into a swimming pool filled with them? It's essential to understand the damage we inflict on ourselves when we dwell in these emotional waters. Why do we stew over things? Why do we obsess over matters we cannot control? It's time to be brutally real with ourselves to avoid playing games with our own well-being. Our thoughts and emotions wield tremendous power over our emotional, mental, and physical health. I think about every one of those belly aches I had and how I realize now how much damage I was doing to my body by allowing myself to be consumed.

Think about a time when nothing ever bothered you. The bottom line: You will never be truly free of the chaos until you free yourself from within the chaos. Beyond unlearning the influences we've absorbed from others, it's crucial to take a hard look at the habits and beliefs we've taught ourselves. Yes, unlearn those self-taught behaviors, thoughts, and feelings that contribute nothing to our happiness. It's not your fault; you did your best with what you had. Many of you lacked the necessary guidance to cope with life's challenges because vital influences like family and friends were absent.

Please, hear this loud and clear: It's not your fault. You don't have to carry that burden anymore. It's been eating away at you, leaving you feeling empty, lonely, alienated, disillusioned, frustrated, and just plain exhausted. Worrying has taken its toll, and it's time to break free from this cycle. Learning to manage anger, shift our outlook on life, or address psychological issues is vital for maintaining a healthy mind.

If you've been the person harboring anger, remember this: the best apology is changed behavior. Forgive yourself and move forward. You can't keep beating yourself up for past mistakes and expect a bright future. If you want change, you'll have to work for it. There is no easy way out.

Now more than ever, you must be the most authentic version of yourself, living your life without evasion. This is not a wish; it's a must-have commitment. Challenge your sense of security, but do not be thoughtless about it. Many of you, like I once did, cling to what you perceive as safe. Embrace the process of revolutionizing yourself, even if instability seems uncomfortable. Change can be unsettling, but remember, someone out there always has it worse.

Remember to ask yourself, "What part of me is being disturbed, and should I really be?" How much do you care about yourself? Do you genuinely love the person in the mirror? Love is an action, not just words. Let it guide your choices and inspire you to embrace your brilliance, not only for your sake but also for those deserving of your love and light.

As we proceed on this profound journey of self-discovery and transformation, remember that facing your emotions and challenging your own limitations is part of the path to a more fulfilled life. Stay tuned for the next chapter, where we'll explore your level of self-belief and your awareness of it.

Chapter 3 Exercise: Master Your Madness

Hey warrior, ready to unleash your inner beast and conquer the chaos within? This exercise is not for the faint-hearted; it's for those hungry for control over their own damn minds.

Anger Audit: Catalog your anger triggers. When do you find yourself boiling over? Is it at work, in relationships, or stuck in traffic? Identify these triggers like a detective solving a case. Awareness is your weapon.

Let Go of the Uncontrollables: List the things in your life you cannot control. Accept it. Own it. Whether it's someone else's actions, the weather, or the traffic jam that hijacks your morning, repeat after me: "I can't control this, and that's okay." Practice letting go.

Positive Affirmation Overdrive: Counteract the negative chatter in your mind with a barrage of positive affirmations. Write down at least five affirmations that combat your most toxic thoughts. Repeat them like a mantra. You are rewiring that brain of yours. This exercise isn't a stroll in the park; it's a battle against the madness within.

Channel that inner warrior, face the chaos, and emerge on the other side victorious. Remember, the mind is a powerful weapon— time to master it. Onward!

CHAPTER 4
WHAT DO YOU BELIEVE ABOUT YOURSELF?

"Self-love is a good thing but self-awareness is more important.
You need to once in a while go 'Uh, I'm kind of an asshole'."
- Louis C.K.

Welcome back, my fellow seekers of self-awareness. In this chapter, we dive deep into the beliefs that shape our lives and drive the decisions we make. You see, our thoughts and beliefs are like architects designing the blueprint of our existence.

Consider this: each of us is the center of our own universe, with a consciousness that is uniquely our own. The beliefs we hold not only govern the steps we take but also fuel the thoughts that drive our decisions.

This is precisely why expanding your self-awareness is crucial. Your thoughts always trace back to the belief systems you have adopted. Yes, adopted! It is a subtle realization that we can change the world as we experience it by changing our belief systems and thoughts.

Your thoughts wield immense power over your life. Recall the last time you were in a bad mood. Did it seem like everything in your life turned unfavorable? "I'm tired, my head hurts, my feet hurt, and I'm working hard, but no one's tipping well!" It may seem like everything and everyone outside of you is to blame, but is it really? Or did you create or attract these circumstances? Now, what if you shifted from that bad mood to a joyous and thankful one? Suddenly, everything outside of you appears to improve.

Understanding your consciousness and being aware of your emotional states on both good and bad days is essential. It sets the stage for reshaping your life.

Allow me to share a story from my own life. In high school, I had an American History teacher named Coach Phil Annarella. On the first day of class, he shared a lesson I've carried with me throughout my life. A classmate asked, "What will be on your tests and quizzes?" Coach Annarella replied, "If I mention a subject more than three times during my lectures, it's likely to be on the quiz or test." I mention this to emphasize that the repeated mention of "self-awareness" in this book is not a test but a vital concept.

Now, let's reflect: Do you genuinely believe that you're always aware and in complete control of your actions and behavior? If you answered yes, take a moment to reconsider. Are you genuinely conscious and in control of your actions and behavior?

If your life is overwhelmed by negativity, I ask you with all the compassion in my heart to dig deep within yourself. Understand the belief systems you've accumulated. Own up to these belief systems that trigger thoughts detrimental to your well-being. These are the beliefs that hold you back, keep you stagnant, and prevent you from achieving more or living the life you desire.

So, why choose to remain in a place you do not want to be? Why do you find comfort in unhappiness and disappointment? Why do you shy away from opportunities for growth and fulfillment? Do you believe you deserve happiness? Do you believe you should expect greatness in your life? Do you believe there is more to life than what you are currently experiencing? Often, it's our belief systems that shape our perspectives and hold us back.

Think about how you think about everything. Understand your perspective and, more importantly, how you arrived there. What's stopping you from taking on more responsibility at work? Did you internalize negative messages that convinced you that you can't do it? What keeps you discouraged even after stepping up? Is it the negative chatter in your break room or, worse, the chatter in your own mind, reinforcing your hopelessness about finding new opportunities?

It's time to recognize that what we believe about ourselves can either empower us or tear us apart. Reflect on your childhood;

were you encouraged or discouraged? These early years set the stage for the accumulation of our belief systems. The beauty is that you have a choice not to perpetuate these beliefs. Continuing to live in your past is akin to stunting your own growth. You don't have to maintain belief systems that no longer serve you. As we grow, we are not obligated to cling to beliefs that stunt our progress.

Start by eliminating the mental waste in your life by revisiting your belief systems. This process gets you closer to understanding and expanding your awareness of your consciousness. It puts you on the path to unlearning behaviors that no longer serve you.

Your past does not define your present, and it certainly does not determine your future. You have the power to redefine what you believe about yourself and your potential. Be honest with yourself and examine what you truly believe. Challenge beliefs that were handed to you and weren't of your own making.

Remember, you cannot live by someone else's beliefs and expect to lead a life of happiness and fulfillment. It's time to stop singing someone else's song about you and compose your own melody. You have the choice to believe or disbelieve what has been told to you, including the stories you tell yourself.

As we continue on this journey, remember that self-awareness and challenging your beliefs are critical steps toward achieving lasting happiness and personal growth. Stay tuned for the next chapter, where we will explore the power of setting intentions and taking action.

Chapter 4 Exercise: Reinvent Your Beliefs

Alright, trailblazer, time to bulldoze through the old and pave the way for a new you. This exercise is for the rebels ready to question everything and redefine their reality.

Belief Breakdown: List three beliefs about yourself that have been holding you back. They are like chains, keeping you anchored. It's time to break them down. Why do you believe them? Where did they come from? Expose the roots.

Affirmation Revolution: Craft three powerful affirmations that challenge those limiting beliefs. These affirmations are not wishy-washy; they are declarations of your new reality. Repeat them daily. Tattoo them on your soul.

Mirror Reinvention: Stand tall in front of that mirror again. Look into your eyes, the windows to your soul. Declare your new affirmations with conviction. You are not asking, you are telling. The mirror reflects the person you are becoming.

This exercise is your wrecking ball, demolishing the old to make way for the new. Embrace the discomfort, challenge those beliefs, and reinvent yourself from the ground up. It is not a makeover, it's a revolution. Get ready to redefine your story. Onward!

CHAPTER 5
THE POWER OF SETTING INTENTIONS AND TAKING ACTION

"Life is one big road with lots of signs. So when you riding through the ruts, don't complicate your mind. Flee from hate, mischief and jealousy. Don't bury your thoughts, put your vision to reality. Wake up and live!" - Bob Marley

Ladies and gentlemen, I want you to understand something profound. Your attention is not just an everyday commodity; it's a sacred force. It's the currency of your consciousness, and you get to decide where it's spent.

In a world brimming with distractions, it is essential to safeguard your attention. Anything that steals your peace, that plunders your serenity, does not deserve a single moment of your precious focus. By preserving your attention, you unlock the secret to drawing in the good things that life has to offer.

Imagine your attention as a beacon, a guiding light that illuminates your path. When you shield it from the chaos, you effortlessly draw in miracles and magical experiences that feed your soul. The Universe responds to your intentions, and as you direct your attention wisely, you pave the way for your deepest desires to manifest.

It all begins by tuning into yourself, by forging a connection with your deepest desires and most profound dreams. With intention as your compass, you set your course, charting a journey that is uniquely yours. And when you commit to what you truly want, regardless of the circumstances, you tap into the boundless reservoir of your own potential.

This commitment isn't just a fleeting wish. It's a resolute promise to yourself, an unshakable decision that you will pursue your dreams, no matter what obstacles stand in your way. It's about setting your sights on a destination and embarking on a journey, one step at a time, even when the path ahead seems daunting.

Let me share a personal revelation that changed the course of my life. At a certain point, I realized that I was merely dreaming about writing a book, and those dreams were slipping through my fingers. Every day that I procrastinated, my book remained an elusive fantasy.

Then came the epiphany – I had to set a clear intention and take decisive action. It was a pivotal moment, a wake-up call to stop postponing my dreams. I declared, "I will write this book, and I will start today." That intention became my guiding star, and I began to write, even if it was just a few paragraphs a day.

It was not always smooth sailing; I encountered moments of doubt and frustration. But each word I penned brought me closer to my goal, and every action I took was a step on the path of realization.

The power of setting intentions is like crafting a roadmap for your desires. It is about defining your goals with precision and creating a plan to achieve them. Intentions are the first spark of creation, the blueprint for the life you wish to lead.

But it's action that breathes life into those intentions, making them tangible and real. It's an action that transforms your dreams into reality. And it's an action, however small, that propels you forward.

Starting small is often the key. You don't need to take giant leaps; sometimes, the tiniest step is all it takes to set the wheels in motion. But here's the golden rule: be consistent. Every day, regardless of how you feel, take that one small action, and the momentum you create will propel you toward your dreams.

This journey of setting intentions and taking action is your path to personal growth and fulfillment. It's the magical alchemy that transforms your desires into reality. As you persist, you will watch your dreams unfold before your eyes.

So, commit to your deepest desires, protect your attention, and unleash the power of intention. Your journey has only just begun, and the best is yet to come. Stay tuned for the next chapter, where we will delve into resilience and overcoming the obstacles that stand in your way.

Chapter 5 Exercise: Command Your Attention

Warrior, it's time to wield the sword of focus and reclaim your attention. This exercise is not for the casual observer; it's for the relentless few ready to seize control of their destiny.

Attention Inventory: Catalog where your attention flows daily. Social media? Endless news feeds? Toxic relationships? Identify the energy vampires stealing your focus. Write them down, acknowledge the culprits.

Sacred Attention Declaration: Draft a manifesto declaring what deserves your sacred attention. What are your priorities? What aligns with your deepest desires? This is not a wish list, it's your battle cry. Be ruthless in what makes the cut.

Miracle Magnetism: Visualize your life when your attention is a magnet for miracles. Close your eyes and vividly picture it. Feel the energy, the joy, the success. This vision is your North Star. Let it guide your attention.

This exercise is not a stroll through distraction-land; it's a battle for your focus. Sharpen that sword, cut through the noise, and declare dominion over your attention. Remember, where attention goes, energy flows. Choose wisely. Charge forth!

CHAPTER 6
YOU NEED TO SAY "FK IT" AND FACE IT**

"I'm just a human being trying to make it in a world that is rapidly losing its understanding of being human." - Rick James

Alright, my warriors, let's dive into one of the most vital facets of personal growth: resilience and overcoming life's relentless obstacles. I've got to admit, this is a topic that sets my heart ablaze with passion, and I hope to ignite that very same fire within you.

Life, as we know it, can be downright frustrating. It tosses curveballs, sends storms our way, and presents us with challenges that test our very limits. It's a harsh but undeniable fact—there are things beyond our control. We cannot dictate the thoughts or actions of others, and external factors often conspire to confound us.

But here's the kicker, my warriors: it's not in controlling these external elements that our power lies, it is in how we respond. We may not hold dominion over the world, but we sure as hell are the masters of our own responses.

When you find yourself in the midst of a storm, you have got to learn to say, "F**k it," and face it head-on. This is not about ignoring the storm or pretending it's not there. It's about summoning the courage to confront it, to wade through the tempest, knowing that on the other side, there's sunlight waiting.

Resilience is not about avoiding life's obstacles; it's about navigating them with grace and strength. The external world may be beyond our command, but our internal world, our response, is where our power thrives.

And how do you harness this power, you might ask? Well, it

starts with stillness—a profound sense of self-awareness that allows you to observe your thoughts without judgment. When you turn inward, you unlock the doors to personal power. It's like finding the switch that illuminates your path in the darkest of times.

In the face of adversity, your ability to set boundaries becomes your shield and your sword. No matter what others say or do, it is your emotional landscape to navigate. This doesn't mean you isolate yourself from the world; it means that you hold the reins of your reactions.

Let go of the toxic habit of obsessing over others' achievements. It's a dead-end road that only leads to discontent. Instead, aim to be better than your past self. You are unique, with a life story that's entirely your own. Comparing yourself to others is like comparing apples to oranges, it's unhelpful and leads to frustration.

Remember, your journey is your own. There is no need to compete with anyone but the person you were yesterday. It is about growth, personal evolution, and the daily pursuit of becoming the best version of yourself.

Cut through the noise of the world, the endless comparisons, and the toxic habits. Focus on what truly matters—your growth, your journey, and your well-being. Cherish your time, for it is a treasure you cannot replenish.

In the grand tapestry of life, obstacles will always emerge. But as we learn to say "F**k it" and face them with determination, as we remember that our response is our greatest power, we rise above.

Stay tuned for the next chapter, where we will explore the art of self-compassion, a crucial element of personal growth and resilience. Remember, my warriors, you've got this.

Chapter 6 Exercise: Embrace the F*ck-It Philosophy

Hell yeah, renegade! Get ready to unleash the power of the "fuck-it" attitude. This exercise is for those who have had enough and are ready to face life head-on with unapologetic determination.

F*ck-It List Creation: It's time to flip the script on the traditional bucket list. Write down things you've been holding back on, fearing judgment or failure. These are now your "F*ck-It" goals. Embrace the audacity.

Bold Action Challenge: Pick one item from your Fck-It list and take immediate, bold action. No tiptoeing. Whether it's starting a side hustle, confronting a toxic relationship, or booking that dream vacation—just fcking do it.

Daily F*ck-It Mantra: Develop a daily mantra embodying the essence of the F*ck-It philosophy. Repeat it in the morning, noon, and night. Let it be the anthem that fuels your fearless approach to life.

This exercise isn't for the timid; it's for the warriors ready to declare, "I'm done playing small!" Embrace the F*ck-It philosophy like armor, charging into battles with a fearless heart. Life's too short for anything less. Onward, fearless soul!

CHAPTER 7
THE ART OF BEING SOULFISH

"The hardest thing to do is to be true to yourself, especially when everybody is watching." - Dave Chappelle

Ladies and gentlemen, it's time for a concept that's crucial to your well-being, one I call "soulfish." Yes, you heard it right, not selfish, but soulfish.

There comes a time in your life when you need to not just get over yourself but let others get over themselves. Yes, you heard me right again. Let them do it by themselves. Let them figure it out themselves. You see, my friends, you cannot fix everything, and you certainly cannot solve every equation in life for everybody. It's a herculean task to manage ourselves, let alone someone else and their issues. Be real with yourself, and for heaven's sake, don't play yourself. You have got to draw the line.

Don't exhaust yourself by trying to work it all out for others all the time. You cannot be the knight in shining armor for everyone you meet. You are not a superhero, and you don't have to save the world. Save more than just a fraction of yourself for yourself.

Too often, we find ourselves entangled in the mess of other people's lives, neglecting our own needs and sanity. You may be the type of person who goes above and beyond, trying to be the solution for everyone, a blessing to all. But in the process, you forget to be the water – to nourish your own soul and quench your own thirst.

The art of being soulfish is not about being callous or indifferent. It's about maintaining a balance, a boundary, and a sense of self-preservation. It's about understanding that your well-being matters too. It's about recognizing that you cannot pour from an empty cup.

Now, don't get me wrong, helping others, being there for your loved ones, and making a positive impact on the world is beautiful. It's part of what makes us human, and it's part of what makes life meaningful. But it should not come at the cost of your own happiness, your own health, and your own sanity.

Sometimes, you have to let people figure things out on their own. You have to allow them to navigate their own paths, make their own choices, and face the consequences of those choices. It's not a sign of selfishness, it's a sign of self-preservation.

In the grand orchestra of life, every instrument has its part to play. You're not obligated to play all the instruments. You have your role, your purpose, and your path. And it is perfectly okay to say, "I'm here to support you, but you've got to do the work yourself."

So, my friends, remember the art of being soulfish. It's a delicate dance between helping others and preserving yourself. Do not exhaust your own light trying to ignite someone else's. Let them find their own flame. Be the water, quench your own thirst, and let your own light shine.

In the next chapter, we will delve deeper into the power of resilience, a quality that's not just a virtue but a necessity in the journey of life. Stay tuned, and keep that soulfish fire burning.

Chapter 7 Exercise: The SOULFISH Revolution

Warrior of the soul, get ready to dive deep into the art of being SOULFISH. This exercise is for those ready to liberate themselves from the burdens of others and embrace the unapologetic pursuit of self-love.

Release the Chains: Identify one area in your life where you've been carrying the weight of someone else's problems. Whether it's a friend's drama or a family member's expectations, pinpoint it. Now, visualize cutting those chains and freeing yourself.

The SOULFISH Pledge: Draft your SOULFISH pledge—a promise to reserve a significant portion of your energy and time for yourself. This is not selfishness, it is self-love. Commit to prioritizing your well-being over unnecessary burdens.

The Empowerment Mirror: Stand before your mirror with newfound strength. Repeat your SOULFISH pledge with conviction. Witness the power of reclaiming your energy, letting go of what does not serve you. This is your revolution.

This exercise is your emancipation proclamation, declaring independence from the weight of others. Embrace the SOULFISH revolution, and let the ripples of self-love transform your life. You are the master of your destiny. Onward, liberated soul!

CHAPTER 8
UNLEASH YOUR INNER RESILIENCE

"Everyone has a plan 'till they get punched in the mouth…"
- Mike Tyson

Get ready, because we're about to dive into a topic that's pure dynamite – resilience. It's not just some fancy word, it's your secret weapon for conquering life's challenges. Life can be a rollercoaster, throwing all sorts of curveballs your way. But guess what? Resilience is your ultimate ticket to ride through it all!

Resilience is not a gift you are born with, it's a power you cultivate. It's like forging a shield, making you tough as nails. When life hits you hard, resilience lets you hit back even harder. It's about turning setbacks into setups, obstacles into opportunities, and defeats into victories.

You see, it's easy to be a champ when life is a smooth sail. But, here's the thing – life isn't always a cakewalk. It can feel like a wrestling match with a heavyweight champ. Yet, that's where resilience steps in.

It's your secret strength, your magic potion. Resilience means you do not break when life throws a punch, you bounce back stronger. It's all about transforming problems into challenges you conquer and setbacks into stepping stones towards your dreams.

Every successful person out there has been knocked down a few times. But here's the cool part – they did not stay down. They used their falls as trampolines to jump even higher. They harnessed the power of resilience.

Now, I've been where you are. Life threw some crazy curveballs at me too. There were moments when I felt like I was in the boxing ring with life itself. But that's when I realized the magic of resilience.

In those tough times, I learned that it's not about how hard life hits you; it's about how hard you can hit back. Life's challenges will not crush you unless you let them. It's not about how many times you fall, it's about how you rise each time – fierce, determined, and unbreakable.

So, here's your mission – when life gets tough, you get tougher. Don't just weather the storm, dance in the rain! See every setback as a dare, a challenge to outdo yourself.

Resilience is your battle cry, your rallying call. It is what makes you a force to be reckoned with. Remember, life doesn't just happen to you, it unfolds for you. The challenges you face are opportunities to unleash your inner warrior.

In our next chapter, we'll explore self-compassion, a practice that is like a superpower for your heart and soul. Get ready, because we're about to ignite the flame of resilience even brighter.

Chapter 8 Exercise: Own Your Resilience with Fire

Firewalker, this exercise is for those ready to stomp through the embers of adversity and emerge as a phoenix. Get ready to ignite the flames of your resilience with unbridled passion.

Resilience Revelation: Reflect on a challenging moment in your life. What seemed insurmountable at the time? Write it down. Now, identify the strength and resilience you discovered within. Acknowledge the fire burning in you.

Phoenix Affirmations: Craft three affirmations embodying the spirit of the phoenix—rising from ashes, stronger than before. These affirmations are your flames of resilience. Let them burn in your mind, reminding you of your unyielding power.

Firewalk Challenge: Metaphorically or literally (if safely possible), embark on a symbolic firewalk. As you tread on the embers, visualize walking through challenges, emerging unscathed. Feel the heat, embrace the discomfort, and triumphantly cross to the other side.

This exercise is not for the faint-hearted, it's for the warriors ready to dance with the flames and emerge unbroken. Own your resilience with the fervor of a blazing inferno. You are the fire and the phoenix—indestructible. Onward, fiery soul!

CHAPTER 9
UNLEASH YOUR SELF-COMPASSION WARRIOR

"No hay nada más fuerte que una persona que se ama a sí misma incondicionalmente." — Gilberto Santa Rosa
(Translation: "There's nothing stronger than a person who loves themselves unconditionally.")

Dear kindred spirits, let's embark on a profound exploration — the gentle embrace of self-compassion. In this sanctuary of understanding, we step away from harsh judgments and instead become our own source of solace, a compassionate companion on life's unpredictable journey.

Imagine those challenging days when the world seems to crumble around you. In these moments, self-compassion is your comforting ally, a soothing voice that resonates like a caring friend offering encouragement in times of struggle.

It's essential to recognize that stumbling, making mistakes, or enduring difficult days is not a testament to weakness but an inherent aspect of our shared human experience. Life is not always a tranquil stroll; it often feels like an arduous journey. Yet, it's amid the trials and tribulations that we find the fertile ground for personal transformation.

Self-compassion is not about dwelling in self-pity or weaving a web of excuses. It's a gentle gaze upon our struggles, pain, and defeats, affirming with sincerity, "I am here with you, facing these challenges head-on."

Quiet that inner critic, that persistent voice that echoes doubts and shortcomings. Life already presents us with a myriad of challenges, we need not add our self-sabotage to the mix. Instead, strive to be your most ardent supporter, a steadfast motivator cheering you through every hurdle.

As you delve into the embrace of self-compassion, a latent power within you will be unveiled – a resilience that allows you to rebound from setbacks, transforming them into propellants for your aspirations.

Picture yourself in a metaphorical heavyweight fight, where life delivers a solid punch that leaves you reeling. What if, instead of succumbing to defeat, you rise again, fortified with an unwavering determination to triumph? This is the essence of the strength ignited by self-compassion.

Your mission is clear – become your own nurturing guide. Envelop yourself with the same tenderness, understanding, and unwavering support you readily extend to those you hold dear. When life's challenges intensify, remind yourself that you possess an innate ruggedness, a resilience ready to weather any storm.

Always remember, self-compassion is not indicative of fragility; rather, it is a testament to extraordinary strength. It's an art, an uplifting force that gently lifts you when the world tries to keep you down.

In our upcoming chapter, we're immersing ourselves in a "Soul Revolution." Prepare to awaken your inner maestro and orchestrate a symphony of positivity in your life. Life is not a mere series of events, it's a profound unfolding. It's time to seize the inherent power within and conquer it all with compassion leading the way.

Chapter 9 Exercise: Cultivating Self-Compassion Moments

Journal Reflections:

Set aside dedicated time in your journal for self-reflection. Acknowledge a recent challenge or mistake without self-judgment.
Write a compassionate letter to yourself, addressing the difficulties you faced. Offer words of understanding and encouragement, as you would to a dear friend.

Daily Affirmations:

Craft daily affirmations centered around self-compassion. Phrases like "I am resilient in the face of challenges," or "I embrace my imperfections with kindness" can serve as uplifting reminders. Repeat these affirmations each morning, allowing them to resonate and guide your mindset throughout the day.

Mindful Breathing:

Practice mindful breathing exercises. In moments of stress or self-criticism, pause and take slow, deep breaths.
With each breath, consciously release self-judgment and replace it with self-compassion. Visualize inhaling calmness and exhaling self-acceptance.

Shared Compassion:

Extend the practice of self-compassion to others. Recognize moments when friends or family face challenges.
Offer words of empathy and understanding, fostering an environment of compassion within your relationships.

Gratitude for Growth:

Reflect on personal growth and resilience. List three instances where you faced adversity and emerged stronger. Express gratitude for the lessons learned through these experiences, recognizing the transformative power of self-compassion.

Remember, the journey of self-compassion is a continuous process, and these exercises aim to nurture that journey with mindful, compassionate practices.

CHAPTER 10
THE MAESTRO OF YOUR EXISTENCE

"In the grand symphony of life, our choices are the instruments, and we are the conductors. Each decision contributes to the masterpiece we're creating." — Beethoven

Alright, fellow architects of destiny, let's cut through the mist and plunge into the essence of self-determination. This is not a casual thought; it's a call to be your own unapologetic, resolute, and unwavering maestro.

Envision this: you've weathered one of those turbulent days when it feels like the universe is staging a revolt. Now, this is where the symphony of self-determination takes center stage. It's akin to a resounding crescendo, a fiery anthem you'd belt out for a friend weathering the same storm.

Understand this — it's perfectly okay to falter, to stumble through blunders, to navigate the darkness of a gloomy day, week, or even a month. Life is not a leisurely stroll through an idyllic park, it's more like an arduous boot camp. But let's get real here: it's the obstacles and skirmishes that transform you into an indomitable force.

Self-determination isn't about wallowing or weaving intricate excuses. It's about locking eyes with your struggles, your pain, your defeats, and boldly declaring, "I'm taking you head-on."

It's about hushing that internal critic, that nagging voice in your mind incessantly murmuring about your imperfections. Life serves up plenty of challenges; you don't need to be your own stumbling block. You must evolve into your greatest cheerleader, your most fervent motivator.

Now, tune in, because once you embrace the symphony of self-determination, you'll unveil a latent power within. It's the power to rebound from any blow, to transmute setbacks into propellants for your aspirations.

Envision this scenario: you're in a heavyweight bout, and life lands a formidable punch that sends you staggering. What's your move? Do you sprawl on the canvas, defeated, and shattered, or do you rise with a newfound ferocity, more resolute than ever to triumph in the match? That's the breed of tenacity, the symphony of self-determination sparks.

So, here's your mandate – become your own orchestral commander. Treat yourself with the same unyielding determination, stern love, and unwavering reinforcement you'd extend to a trusted comrade. When life's cadence becomes rugged, remind yourself that you're robust.

In our next chapter, we're preparing to awaken the maestro within and discover how boundaries can help unleash a tidal wave of positivity in your life. Life isn't a mere occurrence, it's a grand symphony orchestrated for you. It's time to seize the unlimited force within and conquer it all.

Chapter 10 Exercise: Your Life's Symphony: An Elaboration

Visualize Your Masterpiece: Close your eyes. Picture your life as a painting. What's on your canvas? Reflect on where you are right now without judgment. Allow the imagery to unfold like a story.

Select Your Colors: Identify the key elements in your life—relationships, career, health. What colors represent them? Is your palette intentional and vibrant, or is it a bit messy? Choose the colors you want, consciously shaping your narrative.

Plan Your Artistic Journey: What kind of symphony do you want to create? Outline your intentions for the coming months. Be specific. These are the guiding notes for your life's melody. Consider it a roadmap for the next movement in your composition.

Embrace the Challenges: Acknowledge the challenges you face. How can these challenges add depth to your life's story? Embrace them as part of the journey. Each challenge is a plot twist, a turn in the narrative that contributes to the richness of your artistic expression.

Remember, your life is your magnum opus. You are the maestro, conducting the grand symphony of your existence. Seize the brush, pick the colors, and let the symphony of your life resonate with intention and purpose. You're not just an artist, you're the creator of your masterpiece. Embrace it!

CHAPTER 11
THE POWER OF BOUNDARIES

"Your time is limited, don't waste it living someone else's life. Establishing boundaries is the art of protecting your time for what truly matters." — Steve Jobs

Alright, folks, get ready for a deep dive into a game-changer — the mighty force known as boundaries. You've navigated the seas of self-discovery, and now it's time to armor up with the fortress that preserves your sanity.

Ever felt the burnout blues, the aftermath of nodding 'yes' to every beck and call? Your time is as rare and precious as a gemstone, and not everyone deserves a piece of it. Enter boundaries — your proclamation that says, "Hold on, this is my space, my time, my energy, and you don't get to trample all over it."

What holds true significance for you? Your aspirations? Inner peace? Once you've crystalized your priorities, defending them becomes non-negotiable. Envision your boundaries as an impervious force field—nothing breaches it without your explicit permission.

Remember if guilt appears like the annoying mosquito attempting to invade your space, swat it! Your boundaries aren't about excluding others; they're about shielding what's crucial to your well-being.

Let's talk tough love. Mastering the art of saying 'no' is non-negotiable. Saying 'yes' to everything is a fast track to overwhelm. If it doesn't align with your goals, priorities, or mental well-being, it's a firm 'no.' The world won't crumble because you declined a few invitations.

Understanding Boundaries: Boundaries delineate the limits of what is acceptable and unacceptable in your world. They aren't walls; think of them as gates that swing open and closed based on your needs.

Boundaries aren't confined to personal life, they're your secret weapon in the professional arena also. Learn to establish clear expectations at work. You're not a superhero, you can't do it all. But what you can do is excel in what genuinely matters. Consider the following as you now have an improved awareness of boundaries.

Types of Boundaries: Consider physical boundaries (personal space), emotional boundaries (protecting your feelings), and time boundaries (managing your schedule). Each plays a pivotal role in maintaining a harmonious equilibrium.

Guilt and Boundaries: Guilt often accompanies the enforcement of boundaries. It's crucial to recognize that guilt often stems from societal expectations, not your personal limitations. It's okay to safeguard your energy.

The 'No' Muscle: Saying 'no' is not selfish; it's liberating. It's a proclamation that your priorities matter. Practice flexing your 'no' muscle in front of a mirror until it becomes second nature.

Boundary-Setting at Work: In a professional setting, transparent boundaries can pave the way for increased productivity and a healthier work-life balance. Learn to articulate your limits effectively without the fear of repercussions.

As we go deeper into understanding ourselves, you've now mastered the skill of setting boundaries—a crucial tool to protect your time and energy. Think of boundaries as your personal bodyguards, standing firm and saying, "This is my space, my time, and within these limits, I'm in charge."

With your shield of boundaries, you've created a safe haven, shielding yourself from the constant demands of the world. Now, stand tall within these boundaries, knowing you are the one who decides what enters your sanctuary.

Moving forward, let's explore another internal power—the ability to set intentions and take action. Think of it as the next step in understanding yourself, building on what you've learned about boundaries. Get ready for Chapter 12, where we'll dive into "Unleashing Your Inner Power." We'll tap into your resilience, turning setbacks into stepping stones to reach your full potential. Get ready to discover a stronger version of yourself in the next chapter of this incredible journey.

Chapter 11 Exercise: Boundary Bootcamp

Priority Check: Reflect on your top three priorities in life. Write them down to solidify them in your mind.

Energy Drainers: Identify the activities or people draining your energy and hindering your progress.

The Assertive 'No': Practice saying 'no' assertively and without guilt. Imagine scenarios where you confidently decline.

Communication Drill: Choose someone in your life, and communicate your boundaries clearly. Observe their response and reflect.

Remember: Your boundaries are the fortress of your well-being. Guard it fiercely! Life doesn't happen to you; it happens for you. And now, armed with boundaries, you're not just navigating life; you're steering it. Welcome to the Boundary Bootcamp!

CHAPTER 12
UNLEASHING YOUR INNER POWER

"True power is not the ability to control others, but the strength to control oneself. Embrace your principles with a ferocity that intimidates self-doubt." — Lao Tzu

It's time to get brutally honest with yourself and awaken the dormant force within. No more tiptoeing around—your principles aren't suggestions, they're the damn law. Here's the raw, unfiltered truth: it's time to embrace that power with a ferocity that scares off self-doubt.

Your principles aren't wishy-washy ideas, they're the bedrock of your resilience. Imagine your doubts scattering like cockroaches when the lights come on. That's the kind of raw, unfiltered power we're talking about. Dig deep into your core values. Make them vivid; make them living entities ready to fend off the invasive forces of doubt.

Enough with coddling your fears. It's time to manhandle them into the harsh light of day. Name them, confront them, and watch them crumble. Picture each fear as a specter lurking in the shadows. The warrior within you drags them into the spotlight, dissecting their essence until they lose their power.

Resilience isn't just a concept to casually discuss over tea—it's a journey of self-discovery. What's your daily ritual, your personal practice? Whether it's a morning affirmation, a session of mindful movement, or a moment of serene reflection—make it a source of growth. Each experience is a step in building your inner strength. Detail the specific rituals that shape your day. If it's a morning affirmation, describe the emotions it cultivates. If it's exercise, outline how each movement contributes to your physical and mental well-being.

Think of failure not as a setback but as a valuable lesson in your resilience journey. Analyze your defeats with the precision of a seasoned strategist. Describe the process of facing your fears head-on. Picture each setback as a stepping stone, propelling you forward. Instead of shrinking in the face of challenges, use them as momentum towards triumph.

Fear isn't an adversary, it's your guide through uncharted territories. Identify your fears, confront them, and move forward. Consider fear as a mentor, offering guidance through the landscapes of personal growth. Share personal stories where fear acted as a compass rather than a hindrance.

Examine the limitations you've placed on yourself. It's time to break free from those shackles. Comfort zones may be suitable for some, but growth lies beyond familiarity. Emphasize the importance of breaking free as an essential step in your journey.

Craft your anthem—not a melody for the faint-hearted, but a powerful roar for the fierce. Your anthem is the soundtrack to your resilience. Let it be a symphony that resonates through every challenge, reminding you of your strength and ability to overcome.

As we stand at the crossroads of our inner power, ready to unleash a symphony of resilience, the journey takes a transformative turn. Be charged with the raw might of embracing your principles and facing your fears head-on. Upon doing so will ignite flame of gratitude as you remain aware of yourself and how far you have come. In the next chapter we'll dive into power of gratitude and what it can truly do for us.

Chapter 12 Exercise: Inner Power Bootcamp

Daily Empowerment Ritual: Identify a daily ritual that empowers you. It could be a morning affirmation, a physical activity, or a moment of mindfulness.
Commit to practicing this ritual every day for the next week.
Journal about the emotions and changes you observe during this week.

Reflecting on Defeats: Think about a recent setback or failure.
Analyze it from a strategic standpoint—what were the contributing factors, and what lessons can you extract?
Consider how you can turn this setback into a stepping stone for future success.

Fear as a Compass: Identify a fear or challenge you've been avoiding.
Visualize fear as a guiding force, showing you the way forward.
Take a small step towards confronting this fear and record your experience.

Breaking Free Exercise: List three self-imposed limitations or comfort zones that you recognize.
Develop a plan to break free from one of these limitations.
Take the first step this week and document your feelings and observations.

Crafting Your Anthem: Choose a powerful quote, mantra, or affirmation that resonates with your inner power.
Turn it into a personal anthem—something you can repeat to yourself in challenging moments.
Share this anthem with someone close to you and discuss its significance.

CHAPTER 13
THE POWER OF GRATITUDE: CULTIVATING APPRECIATION IN DAILY LIFE

Gratitude unlocks the fullness of life. It turns what we have into enough, and more. It turns denial into acceptance, chaos to order, confusion to clarity. It can turn a meal into a feast, a house into a home, a stranger into a friend." — Melody Beattie

In the fabric of our lives, gratitude is the thread that stitches together the ordinary and the extraordinary. It's more than a fleeting emotion, it's a profound practice that has the potential to reshape our existence. As we embark on this exploration of gratitude, our aim is not just to understand its essence but to embrace it as a transformative force, capable of enhancing our mental well-being and enriching our daily experiences.

Gratitude is the lens through which we perceive the world. I used to hear this often, "Hey Shannon how do you do it, you know feel good almost all of the time?" It's about acknowledging and valuing the positive aspects of our lives, no matter how small or seemingly insignificant. This mindset shift redirects our focus from scarcity to abundance, from what's lacking to what's present. Gratitude invites us to recognize the richness embedded in every moment, making the ordinary truly extraordinary.

Gratitude is more than an attitude, it's a fundamental shift in perspective. It doesn't negate life's challenges but reframes our response to them. When we cultivate gratitude, we consciously choose to see beyond difficulties, finding joy in small victories and beauty in the journey. It's a choice to appreciate the present and anticipate the future with a positive outlook.

One of the wonders of gratitude is its ability to elevate the mundane to the extraordinary. It's not reserved for grand events or momentous occasions. Instead, gratitude magnifies the significance of everyday moments. A shared meal becomes a feast when we appreciate the effort behind it, and a humble abode transforms into a sanctuary when we recognize the warmth and love within its walls.

While gratitude's emotional impact is profound, its tangible benefits are supported by scientific research. In this chapter, we'll unravel the intricate ways in which gratitude rewires our brains. From fostering positivity to enhancing overall well-being and even influencing physical health, the scientific exploration of gratitude adds another layer to its transformative nature. You see, it is more than just being happy.

Gratitude isn't just a passive state, it's an active practice that can be cultivated. This chapter introduces a variety of practical exercises designed to integrate gratitude into your daily life. From keeping a gratitude journal to expressing thanks to those around you, these exercises provide concrete steps to make gratitude a living part of your routine.

Embark on this journey into the heart of gratitude, where philosophy meets practicality. Our exploration isn't merely about understanding gratitude; it's an invitation to actively engage in transformative practices. As we delve into practical exercises, the goal is not only to comprehend but to experience gratitude. It's time to cultivate appreciation in daily life and witness the profound changes that this practice can bring to our mental and emotional well-being.

Chapter 13 Exercise: Cultivating Gratitude

Gratitude Journaling: Set aside a few minutes each day to reflect on and jot down three things you're grateful for. Be specific and delve into the details. It could be a small gesture, a moment of connection, or a personal achievement. Over time, review your entries to witness the accumulation of positive moments.

Expressing Gratitude to Others: Identify someone in your life whom you appreciate but haven't expressed gratitude to recently. Write a heartfelt note, send a message, or share your feelings in person. Be sincere and specific about what you value in them. Notice the impact this act of gratitude has on both you and the recipient.

Gratitude Meditation: Find a quiet space, sit comfortably, and close your eyes. Reflect on aspects of your life you're grateful for, focusing on the sensations associated with this gratitude. Let these feelings permeate your mind, fostering a sense of warmth and positivity.

Gratitude Jar: Designate a jar for your gratitude practice. Regularly write notes about things you're thankful for and place them in the jar. During challenging times, revisit these notes to uplift your spirits and gain perspective.

Gratitude Walk: Take a mindful walk, paying attention to your surroundings. Acknowledge and express gratitude for the elements of nature, the weather, or the simple pleasure of movement. This practice connects you to the present moment and instills a sense of appreciation.

Three Good Things: Before bedtime, recall three positive events or experiences from your day. Reflect on why each event was meaningful or brought you joy. This exercise helps shift your focus to the positive aspects of your daily life.

Random Acts of Kindness: Engage in acts of kindness without expecting anything in return. These acts can be small, such as holding the door for someone or offering a compliment. Reflect on the positive impact of spreading kindness and notice the reciprocal feelings it generates.

Integrate these exercises into your routine to weave gratitude into the tapestry of your life. The transformative power of gratitude lies not just in understanding its concept but in actively engaging with these practices to enrich your daily experiences.

CHAPTER 14

THE WISDOM OF REFLECTION: UNVEILING SELF-DISCOVERY THROUGH INTROSPECTION

"Knowing yourself is the beginning of all wisdom." — *Aristotle*

In the relentless rhythm of modern living, we often find ourselves entangled in the external world, leaving little room for introspection. Yet, in the stillness of reflection, we discover the profound wisdom that resides within. This chapter extends an earnest invitation to embark on a transformative journey of self-discovery through the practice of introspection.

In a world filled with noise, intentional silence becomes a sanctuary for self-exploration. Pause for a moment, let the echoes of your own thoughts be your guide. As you navigate the corridors of your mind, you'll unveil layers of understanding that can shape the course of your life. I recall one time being thrown into a state of introspection after a conversation with my father. He shared his observations of me as a man and reminded me that I need to define the change I want to see in me.

Self-discovery is akin to peeling back the layers of an onion, revealing the core essence. We'll delve into the depths of your values, those fundamental principles that serve as the compass for your actions. What you hold dear has a profound impact on your decisions, relationships, and overall well-being.

Our beliefs, often ingrained from early experiences, influence every facet of our lives. This chapter challenges you to scrutinize those beliefs—about yourself, others, and the world. By understanding the origins of your beliefs, you gain the power to reshape them, aligning them with the authentic narrative you wish to embody.

As we navigate the tapestry of self-discovery, aspirations emerge as vibrant threads. What dreams have you tucked away? What aspirations stir in the recesses of your heart? Visualization becomes a potent tool to breathe life into these aspirations, transforming them from distant desires to tangible goals.

Self-reflection is not a one-time event, it's a continuous journey. Embrace it as a practice, a ritual that brings you closer to your authentic self. The exercises that follow are not assignments but companions on this journey, designed to deepen your connection with the wisdom within. As you immerse yourself in these practices, remember that the destination is not a fixed point but a dynamic evolution of the self.

Through introspection, you unravel the layers, revealing the authentic self beneath. This process requires courage, honesty, and a willingness to confront the shadows. As you navigate the exercises and affirmations ahead, envision the emergence of a more self-aware, resilient, and empowered version of yourself.

Prepare to delve into the exercises, for they are the keys that unlock the doors to your inner sanctum. The journey of introspection is both profound and personal, and in embracing it, you embark on a path of self-discovery that has the potential to reshape the narrative of your life.

Chapter 14 Exercise: Introspection

Values Clarification Exercise: Identify the core values that guide your life. Reflect on how well your current actions align with these values. Consider any adjustments needed to live in greater harmony with your values.

Belief System Analysis: Examine your beliefs about yourself, others, and the world. Question the origins of these beliefs and their impact on your life. Challenge and reshape beliefs that no longer serve your growth.

Aspirations Visualization: Picture your ideal life in vivid detail—personal and professional. Break down long-term aspirations into actionable steps. Create a visual representation of your aspirations to reinforce your commitment.

Prompts for Introspection: What moments in your life have shaped your values? How have your beliefs influenced your major life decisions? What aspirations have you set aside and why? In what areas of your life do you feel the most authentic?

Preparing for the Journey Ahead: As you engage in these exercises and reflect on the prompts, anticipate the unfolding of a journey that transcends the pages of this book. Self-discovery is not a destination, it's a continuous voyage. The exercises and affirmations that follow are not mere tools; they are companions on your odyssey of growth and understanding. Embrace the wisdom that emerges, for within it lies the compass to navigate the course of your extraordinary life.

CHAPTER 15
LIMITLESS FREEDOM PRACTICES

"The most courageous act is still to think for yourself. Aloud. Step into the boundless freedom of your thoughts and let them soar."
— *Coco Chanel*

Greetings, fellow journeyers on the path of self-discovery. As we delve into the depths of our inner landscape, let us embrace the boundless freedom that lies within the caverns of our souls.

Within you exists an inner sanctuary, a realm of tranquility that remains untouched by the chaos of the external world. This realm needs to be maintained. Our journey today involves rediscovering this sacred space and some practices to help maintain your presence there.

Practice: The Inner Sanctuary Meditation
Close Your Eyes: Begin by gently closing your eyes, turning your awareness inward.

Deep Breath In, Deep Breath Out: Take a deep breath in, allowing the air to fill your lungs. As you exhale, release any tension, or worries.

Visualize the Sanctuary: Envision a serene sanctuary within your being. It could be a lush garden, a quiet beach, or any place that resonates with peace.

Feel the Peace Within: Immerse yourself in the tranquility of this inner sanctuary. Feel the peace radiating from the core of your being.

Explore Your Inner Sanctuary: Take a stroll within, exploring the beauty of your sanctuary. Notice the details—the colors, the sounds, the sensations.

Return with Gratitude: When you're ready, return from your inner sanctuary, carrying the serenity with you. Express gratitude for this sacred space within.

Life unfolds as a dance, a rhythmic flow of experiences. Our task is not to resist the dance but to become avid dancers, moving with the ever-changing cadence of existence.

Practice: The Dance of Presence
Flowing Awareness: As you go about your day, cultivate a flowing awareness. Be present with each activity, each interaction, and each breath.

Observe Thoughts as Passersby: Treat your thoughts as passersby in this grand dance. Observe them without attachment, letting them flow in and out of your consciousness.

Surrender to the Present Moment: In the dance of life, surrender to the present moment. Allow it to carry you, trusting the rhythm of existence.

Express Your Dance: At some point in the day, physically express your dance. It could be a literal dance, a walk, or any movement that feels like an expression of your presence.

Amidst the dance, there lies a profound stillness. It is in the embrace of this stillness that we discover the essence of our being.

Practice: The Stillness Meditation

Sit in Silence: Find a comfortable seat. Close your eyes and sit in silence.

Focus on Your Breath: Direct your attention to the breath. Feel the inhalation and exhalation without manipulating it.

Merge into Silence: Gradually, let your awareness merge into the silence between breaths. Rest in this stillness.

Extend the Stillness: After the meditation, carry the stillness with you. Let it infuse your actions and responses throughout the day.

Practice: Reflection on Inner Freedom and Stillness

I recall a time when I was not worrying about my future, I was obsessing about my past mistakes. When I was not thinking about other people's opinions, I spent sleepless nights ruminating over that one thing I did years ago.

These habits lead to a lot of noise in my mind. It became harder for me to think clearly or feel at ease in my life about anything.

Yes, past experiences have an impact on your habits and behaviors, but ultimately you have the ability to choose how you want to show up in the present.

Practice: Breathe and let go.

You have to consciously work towards creating a more peaceful life. Our emotions can cause us to overlook many crucial details when making decisions to do better and feel better.

We must rise above our emotional reactions to perceive the situation as accurately as possible.

Get enough rest and take time to really understand what you are doing. Put time in feeling better first then move forward with making your life choices. Do not waste your time manifesting everything you DO NOT want because your mental space is not clear.

You just have to wait. The emotions will subside on their own. Think about the pros and cons of the choices you make. Practice pausing to avoid reacting impulsively under the influence of strong emotions.

When you're feeling overwhelmed, you tend to say or do things that are not helpful for you.

It's important to be patient with yourself as you let your emotions flow through you. Slow down. Don't remain fixated on how you "should" feel.

Don't judge your emotions. Just breathe through them and let them run their natural course. Once you learn to let your feelings flow, you will experience real freedom.

You will gain the courage to confront difficult emotions and navigate life's challenges with greater peace and clarity.

CHAPTER 16
EMPOWER YOUR FUTURE: A BLUEPRINT FOR RENEWAL AND PLANNING

"You may not control all the events that happen to you, but you can decide not to be reduced by them." — Maya Angelou

As we stand at the edge of this final chapter, take a moment to reflect on the incredible journey you've been through. This is not just an ending; it's a celebration of your growth and strength. Let's dive into the heart of your transformative adventure.

Think back to the beginning, where we started exploring your inner self. The mirror wasn't just a mirror, it was a way to understand who you are. Now, take a moment to sit quietly and think about your journey.

Capture Your Growth: Grab your pen and let it dance across the pages of your journal. Write down how you've changed—your thoughts, beliefs, and actions. See the transformation in your own words.

Sketch Your Journey: Don't just draw a timeline; create something special. Mark the big moments and tough choices that shaped your journey. Celebrate the good times, learn from the challenges, and honor the moments that led to growth.

Share Gratitude: In your journal, write down all the things you're thankful for. Be grateful for the gift of understanding yourself—the good and not-so-good parts.

Activate Your Strength: Life's journey needs strength—think about the times when you said, "I will face it, not evade it."

Move Your Body: Do something physical that shows your strength. Feel your movement declaring to the world that you are strong.
Speak Strength: Write down powerful statements that show your strength. Speak them out loud, reinforcing your unbroken spirit.

Free Yourself: Close your eyes and imagine letting go of past challenges. Picture yourself free and ready for what's next.

Live Honestly: Our journey is all about being real. This chapter is a call to make self-care a priority and stay true to who you are.

Create Your Self-Care Code: List down simple rules for taking care of yourself in your journal. What will guide you in everyday choices?

Use Symbols: Draw pictures or symbols that remind you to be true to yourself. Let them guide you quietly.

Make It a Habit: Include your self-care code in your daily life. Let it be your guide through the ups and downs.

Celebrate Your Wisdom: Let's look back at each chapter, celebrating the good times, learning from challenges, and recognizing how much you've grown.

Feel Each Lesson: Think about the lessons you've learned. Which ones still matter to you? What has become a part of who you are?

Say Thanks: Be thankful for all the lessons—the good, the tough, and the victories.

Look to Tomorrow: Imagine what comes next in your life. Picture yourself moving forward with new self-awareness, strength, and staying true to yourself.

This chapter is the essence of your transformative journey. Your story shows the strength inside you and the real person you've become. As you step into the unknown, remember that the power to shape your life is within you.

Life brings surprises and chances for positive changes. Even in tough times, there's always hope. Open yourself to new possibilities beyond your imagination. Consider taking steps to update your life's journey and plan a New Trip

Think of life as a big adventure. Consider the emotional baggage you carry—beliefs about yourself, old burdens, and unfinished business. Don't let it weigh you down. Rethink your journey. Has it been helpful or hard?

Pack Smartly: Check your emotional baggage. Keep what helps you, and let go of what doesn't.

Plan Mindfully: Plan your life journey carefully. Pack experiences, relationships, and achievements that fit where you want to go.

Letter to Past Self: Write a letter to your past self. Talk about challenges, thank yourself for being strong, and look forward to the future.

Plan for Tomorrow: Picture the person you want to be and think of steps to become that person.

Dear Seeker of Self, as you embark on this remarkable journey of renewal and planning, each intentional step brings you closer to a life loaded with authenticity and purpose. Although the path may have twists and turns, your reservoir of courage and self-awareness will guide you with unwavering steadiness. Sense the exhilaration as you contemplate the unwritten chapters awaiting your unique story. This adventure is yours to shape, and with each decision, you are architecting the destiny that aligns with your deepest aspirations. Embrace the unknown with confidence, for within you resides the power to sculpt a narrative that reflects the essence of your true self. May this journey be a continuous evolution, a symphony of growth, and an enduring celebration of the resilient, authentic warrior that you've become.

In your transformative journey, every experience, whether triumphant or challenging, has shaped your resilience. Each trial, fear conquered, and moment of self-discovery has contributed to the person you've become.

Think about the pages you've turned, each filled with revelations, struggles, and triumphs. Your story is not just a linear progression, it's a testament to your ability to evolve. Every word carries the weight of your resilience, and every chapter turned is a proclamation of your inner strength.

In life your existence can be echoed with the courage to face the unknown, the wisdom to embrace authenticity, and the strength to unleash your inner power.

As you close this chapter and approach the unwritten horizon, remember that the power to transcend, renew, and plan for a future brimming with possibilities is a gift you've given yourself. Embrace it fully, for within you lies the boundless potential to script a narrative that defines not only who you are but who you aspire to become. The canvas is yours, the ink is in your hands, and the story unfolds with each step into the limitless expanse of your own making.

Please know that I am truly proud of you.

CHAPTER 17
AFFIRMATIONS FOR TRANSFORMATION

"WITH EVERY AFFIRMATION, YOU WRITE THE SCRIPT OF YOUR OWN DESTINY." — DEEPAK CHOPRA

It's essential to understand affirmations and the significant role they can have in shaping our thoughts and actions. Affirmations go beyond mere words; they serve as powerful declarations that influence our mindset and, consequently, our reality. Consider them as practical tools for self-improvement, guiding us towards cultivating a more positive and resilient outlook. Think of these affirmations as seeds planted in the fertile soil of our minds, growing into a landscape of self-love and boundless potential. The affirmations ahead are here to walk beside you on your journey, acting as gentle reminders of your inner strength and the vast possibilities within. Incorporate them into your daily routine, allowing them to construct the foundation for the authentic and fulfilling life you aspire to build.

1. I am the architect of my destiny.
2. I release the weight of my past and embrace the freedom of my future.
3. Every challenge is an opportunity for growth. I welcome them with an open heart.
4. I am resilient, and each setback is a stepping stone to my success.
5. My journey is a continuous evolution, and I embrace change with courage and grace.
6. I trust in my ability to create positive outcomes in any

situation.

7. My authenticity is my greatest strength. I am true to myself in every moment.

8. I am worthy of love, success, and all the blessings life has to offer.

9. My thoughts create my reality, and I choose to focus on positivity and abundance.

10. I am a beacon of light, inspiring others with my courage and authenticity.

11. Every breath is an opportunity to start anew. I am present and mindful in each moment.

12. I trust the process of life and allow it to unfold in perfect harmony.

13. I am deserving of all the joy, success, and fulfillment life has to offer.

14. I let go of fear and embrace the boundless possibilities that lie ahead.

15. I am the master of my thoughts, and I choose to cultivate a positive and empowering mindset.

16. My inner strength is a constant source of empowerment.

17. With each passing day, my confidence grows stronger.

18. I am a magnet for positive energy and attract all that I desire.

19. I radiate love and compassion to myself and others.

20. My mind is clear, focused, and capable of achieving greatness.

21. I am open to receiving abundance in all areas of my life.

22. Every challenge I face is an opportunity to learn and improve.

23. I trust in the wisdom of my intuition and make decisions with clarity.

24. My heart is a reservoir of gratitude, and I am thankful for each moment.

25. I release all resistance and go with the flow of the universe.

26. My actions align with my values, bringing harmony to my life.

27. I am a vessel of creativity, and my ideas flow effortlessly.
28. I am a beacon of light, inspiring others to embrace their true selves.
29. I forgive myself and others, freeing my spirit from resentment.
30. I am deserving of love, respect, and all the goodness life has to offer.
31. My potential is limitless, and I am capable of achieving my dreams.
32. I am a source of positivity, uplifting those around me.
33. I release the need for perfection and embrace my authentic self.
34. I am a magnet for miracles, and my life is filled with wonderful surprises.
35. I attract meaningful relationships that nurture and support me.
36. My body is a temple, and I treat it with love and nourishment.
37. I am surrounded by opportunities, and I seize them with confidence.
38. My path is divinely guided, and I trust the journey ahead.
39. I let go of comparison and celebrate the unique essence of who I am.
40. I am a source of kindness, compassion, and understanding.
41. I am grounded, centered, and at peace with the present moment.
42. My life is a canvas, and I paint it with the colors of joy and fulfillment.
43. I release any fear of the unknown and embrace the adventure of life.
44. I am resilient, and I bounce back from challenges with strength and grace.
45. I attract positive and uplifting experiences into my life.
46. My journey is a sacred dance of growth and self-discovery.
47. I am a co-creator of my reality, shaping it with intention and purpose.

48. I am a source of inspiration for myself and others.
49. I welcome change as a catalyst for growth and transformation.
50. My thoughts are seeds of greatness, and I plant them with intention.
51. I trust in the unfolding of my destiny and surrender to divine timing.
52. I am a warrior of self-love, embracing my worthiness and uniqueness.
53. My words have power, and I speak with kindness and positivity.
54. I am aligned with the energy of abundance, and prosperity flows to me.
55. I am a master of my emotions, responding with love and understanding.
56. I let go of any limitations and embrace the boundless possibilities of life.
57. My heart is a sanctuary of peace, and I carry tranquility wherever I go.
58. I am a vessel of joy, spreading laughter and happiness to those around me.
59. My dreams are valid, and I pursue them with passion and determination.
60. I am a channel of divine wisdom, and guidance flows effortlessly to me.
61. I am a magnet for success, and I attract opportunities that align with my purpose.
62. I celebrate my achievements, big and small, with gratitude and joy.
63. I am a force of positive change, contributing to the betterment of the world.
64. I release any self-doubt and step into my power with confidence.
65. I am a guardian of my energy, surrounding myself with positivity and love.
66. My soul is on a journey of expansion, and I embrace the

lessons it brings.

67. I am a source of strength for myself and others during challenging times.

68. I let go of the past, live fully in the present, and embrace the future with hope.

69. I am a beacon of resilience, weathering life's storms with grace and courage.

70. I am a constant learner, growing and evolving with each experience.

71. I am a co-creator of my destiny, manifesting my desires with intention.

72. I am at peace with the flow of life, trusting in its divine orchestration.

73. I am a vessel of love, radiating compassion to all beings.

74. I am a magnet for positive relationships, attracting those who uplift and inspire.

75. I am a source of love and light, contributing to the collective well-being.

76. I am aligned with the energy of the universe, and everything is unfolding perfectly.

77. I am grateful for the journey of transformation, and I embrace the path ahead with joy.

REFLECTIONS AND QUESTIONS

Take a moment for self-reflection with these questions. Grab a pen or simply ponder them. Your answers hold the key to unlocking new insights and positive change in your life. Are you ready to explore your inner world and emerge stronger than ever?

Journey of Self-Discovery: Reflect on a moment from your life when you felt a profound sense of self-discovery. What triggered this realization, and how did it shape your perspective?

Navigating Challenges: Consider a challenging situation you faced. How did you overcome it, and what did you learn about yourself in the process? How can these insights guide you in future challenges?

Defining Moments: Identify three defining moments in your life. What lessons did you extract from each, and how have they contributed to your personal growth?

Personal Values: Examine your core values. How do these values influence your decisions, and in what ways do they align with the principles discussed in the book?

Embracing Change: Share an experience where you embraced change willingly. How did this impact your life, and what strategies can you apply to approach change with a positive mindset?

Relationships and Connections: Reflect on a significant relationship in your life. How has it evolved, and what role has it played in your journey towards self-discovery and personal growth?

Creating Balance: Consider the balance between various aspects of your life—career, relationships, personal well-being. How can you ensure harmony in these areas to foster holistic growth?

A LETTER TO THE FUTURE SELF

Embark on a transformative journey as you craft a letter to your future self. Capture the essence of your present insights, incorporating the wisdom and lessons gained from this book. Seal the letter and tuck it away for a year. When you revisit it, witness the growth and evolution that unfolds, realizing the profound impact of your journey within. Your words today become a powerful compass guiding you toward a future illuminated by newfound understanding and personal transformation. If you don't know what to say, consider the following to ensure writing a good letter:

Goals and Aspirations: Describe the goals and aspirations you currently hold. How do you envision achieving them, and what steps can your future self take to move closer to these aspirations?

Learnings from the Present: Share insights gained from the present moment. What principles and practices from the book do you want your future self to prioritize for continued personal growth?

Overcoming Challenges: Anticipate potential challenges your future self might face. Offer advice on how to navigate these challenges based on the resilience strategies discussed in the book.

Celebrating Achievements: Envision your future self celebrating significant achievements. What milestones do you hope to reach, and how will you acknowledge and appreciate these successes?

Daily Practices: Outline daily practices that contribute to your well-being. How can your future self enhance or modify these practices to align with evolving needs and circumstances?

Maintaining Balance: Consider the balance between ambition and self-care. How will your future self strike a balance between pursuing goals and prioritizing mental, emotional, and physical health?

Reflection on Growth: Reflect on the growth you anticipate for your future self. How will this growth influence your relationships, mindset, and overall quality of life?

DISCUSSION QUESTIONS FOR BOOK CLUBS

Gather with fellow seekers of growth and initiate meaningful conversations. The following discussion questions are designed to fuel thoughtful dialogues within book clubs. Share perspectives, exchange ideas, and collectively explore the depths of the book's transformative concepts.

Impactful Insights: Share a personal insight from the book that resonated with you the most. How has this insight influenced your perspective or actions?

Application in Real Life: Discuss instances where you applied principles from the book in your real life. What changes did you observe, and how did it impact your well-being?

Favorite Chapter or Concept: Identify your favorite chapter or concept from the book. Why did it stand out to you, and in what ways do you plan to integrate it into your life?

Challenges and Growth: Share a personal challenge you faced and the growth you experienced as a result. How did the book contribute to your ability to navigate challenges?

Connection to Others: Explore how the book's principles can foster stronger connections with others. How can implementing these principles improve relationships in personal and professional spheres?

Overcoming Limiting Beliefs: Discuss strategies for overcoming limiting beliefs, as outlined in the book. Share personal experiences or insights on how challenging these beliefs led to personal growth.

Future Application: Consider future scenarios where the book's teachings can be applied. How do you envision using these principles to navigate upcoming challenges or opportunities?

ABOUT THE AUTHOR

Meet Shannon Douglas, a seasoned Governance, Risk, and Compliance professional with over two decades of experience, specializing in identifying and mitigating technology and information security risks. An alumnus of Wilberforce University, Shannon's educational journey has fortified his foundation, contributing to his professional achievements and commitment to lifelong learning.

Beyond the corporate realm, Shannon is a dedicated advocate for personal growth and resilience, bringing a unique blend of professional acumen and personal inspiration to his work and writings. Join him on a journey that transcends the complexities of governance and risk management, exploring the realms of personal development and impactful transformations.

FEEL FREE TO REACH OUT AND STAY CONNECTED

WWW.GOWITHINYOU.COM